in search of
the perfect pair of shoes

miriam owen

In Search of the Perfect Pair of Shoes
is another Bobtimystic Books project.

Copyright © 2016 by Miriam Owen

All rights reserved. This book may not be reproduced or transmitted in any form whatsoever without permission in writing from the author.

Cover design, photography & editing
by Bob Makela

Art
by Miriam Owen

Shoe sketch
by Will Owen

ISBN-13: 978-0692558010
ISBN-10: 0692558012
Manufactured in the United States of America
Third Edition

To order this book or to contact the publisher go to:

www.BobtimysticBooks.com

Suggested retail price: **$15.00**

*And we are pioneers
longing for our freedom*

Thanks to Bob and Molly, who cared enough to think of putting this stuff into one readable piece.

If time is an imaginary thing
then what about

    "putting in your time"   ?

What about "waiting"   ?

Do you take time to wait?
This may be the key to open the gate.

    * * *

I got my feet
up now

He gets the motel fever when he's
                on the move
He gets the motel fever, 'cause
                it makes him groove
To have his entire family gather
                'round the tube
Being lazy in a clean motel.

He's got the motel fever running in
                his blood
And when he hits the road
                it really starts to flood
His eyes keep on a' wandering
                from side to side
Why can't we stop? I'm getting tired
                of this ride.
He's got the motel fever flowing
                deep inside
And when it rises to get him, he
                can only sigh
And take his crazy antics to a
                cheap motel
Forget the destination, this motel
                is swell!

                              May
                              1978

Reached a point
where I cannot tell
dream from reality
   very well
& when I can
   (if I can)
what does it have to do with the mirror?
why do I have to judge myself with the mirror?
& what is the true mirror of the mind?
   expectation
   spontaneous reaction
   lasting affection
   affection of any kind

mirrors of glass
reflections that never last
mirrors of mind
where imaginary shined
a silly little book
but take another look
go not in vain to mirrors
where you nothing ever find.
   Show me to the true mirror
   I think I've been blind
   If you give me that mirror
   I'll leave the other mirrors
              behind.

July
1979

Oh what happens in the
  sands of time
  As we move back & forward,
  opening self to an upward climb
  or staying in the fields of clover
Oh what! maybe they're
the same — I'd better
look it over.

***

Clean, clear, & always painful
I feel the ocean
pouring over everything
I try to put in time
There is no answer here
Just something long before thee
   Beckoning
   But never what I try.

***

Young women believe in earnest
what older women have already seen to be untrue
The beauty of that stage
    being forgotten by older women

Passes in review & again
    seems true to the men who loved them
thinking the older women blue
& sometimes leaving them in their later years
  the younger women to woo

***

The thing is the same
there is much you must uncover
whether wallowing in the fields of pain
or taking yourself above her
  Under divides the heart against
   the things it thinks are wonder
Unto the mounting steps of reign
  which throw faulty cause asunder

***

<u>Love Brother</u>
He carries his lover with him
   everywhere he goes
It already is alright he says
   & he knows
But I got a headache
   from tryin to stay up on my toes
Then you better get down
      — says my lover —

      He'll come & empty your cup
So you can follow him
         to the ends of the earth
No pain in his 2nd birth
    love brother
He'll give me another chance
He won't measure what I'm worth
He'll just keep me in love —
        my love brother.

Jack — airport — early '80s

   Move a straight line
in any direction
as you round the circle
you'll see the reflection
   But leaping the circles
you won't get around
pass back through the middle
   original sound

For regeneration
you ride your own talent
   your special gift
   & you know your own horse
who will lope through
      the middle
as you solve the riddle
in the great expectation of
    staying on course.

***

Eleanora the whiz woman
   Lean & lanky stride
In constant occupation
   Lets her eager efforts glide
She sideward folds the laundry
   While you're standing on her porch
She watches you with wandering eye
   While sitting on the couch.
She'll up & bake a super-cake
   While others sit round talking
She'll quote you a statistic
   In psychologic mocking
She comes upon you unawares
   And gives you good advice
I wonder if she takes her own
   She surely keeps apace —
But I have watched her
         gliding off
On her escapes to space.

***

How can we know so little?
   You know what you can prove
The scientist takes his dreams
                    into the lab
       from out of the blue
He walks alone, from time on time
His thoughts in doubt
                        ascending
   the path the others later go
On his frontier depending.

             ***

  Exotic woman from the
        magazine world
Do you go with the gypsy Davey?
Do you ride in the wagon
  with umbrella top
  cook him his bread & his gravy?
Do you make him his fire
  at his every stop
Help him in picking each
        season's ripe crop
Then go out to the streets
        of new cities to shop
To seek treasure in each new
        army-navy?

'79

I made my little Molly feel so bad
she couldn't do the needle work
& then I found I couldn't do it either
no wonder it was so hard to do
   a perfect line across for Molly
   if it wasn't even easy for her mother.

***

What about the shield
& the two-edged sword, Lord?
What about the old forgotten
    once adored?

What kind of a good shepherd
  would lead his sheep astray?
What kind of a good shepherd
  wouldn't even know his own way?
Am I in the wheat field, grinding?
a double-minded man?

release me from this question

   —   if you can

'79

I believe in something
It is not superstition
& I expect to see it
Why not before I die?
I expect to focus on a high supernal feeling
But I think I should be able
   to see it in a way I can't deny

God should really show me
   in a way I'm understanding
The way to walk the road
       that my obedience is demanding.

***

<u>Relocation Station</u>
The actor takes his best cat
    out of the bag
& offers it up for your
      inspection.

Are you getting a true reflection?

Is what's there in your delection
      a true reflection?

  or miscreation, misrecollection
    lost in action
    vacant direction
    another faction
    pure elation
 no base station
    relocation

1979

You tell me how a person is able to
return to the school books
after "For Your Love"
has come vibrating over the waves
of his RCA Victor clock radio.
For your love, oh I would do
anything, I would do anything
for your love. Somehow it
has become difficult to believe
that sinking sadly back into the
numbers & vocabulary & science
charts measures up to what you
now know you have to find out about.
Once you have heard the sound,
you can never go back to
twinkle twinkle little star & feel
the same way. You wonder after
normal everyday life has been thus
replaced by the hope of bliss
whether you have broken a
commandment & committed adultery.

But you were not responsible.
It just appeared there
through the air
into your ear

But you were not responsible.
It just appeared there

through the air
  into your ear
  into your body
  & from that time on
it is just never like it
was before.

It hit different
  people differently, but it
  hit them all. It
was a complete change of breath
  practice, you might say in
contemporary religious terms.

There was "Now & For Always,"
                            ones like
"No One Knows" & "Go Now,
            Be My Baby"
& it would be like a drug on that
  sound for awhile.
& always in the cars, we
  would switch the stations around
  & our mothers would let us, &
then the record store inside the
little booths with 45s you
could play & not even buy.
You might play 12 & buy one —
89¢.

It was an all consuming
climate. Don't doubt it. For
 people who had any kind of
dry existence at all, the
drink of rock & roll was soon
more than great relief — it became
the milk of infants being born
into the land of inner consciousness
& there was no returning by choice.

what was happening was not good or bad.
It just was. You had many who
were more four square & could
stay in sports or academics or clubs,
but huge numbers were thrown
off balance to search irretrievably
the ocean of feeling flooding up
behind them as rock & roll
broke open to the white masses
the sounds now evolving out
of black gospel music. I was
one of these. The sounds were
evocative of places in the mind
& heart most middle class
teenagers had never visited before.

Their family culture had simply not
 prepared them to confront these
feelings & remain in a mind

to continue playing monopoly.
    It was just too new. It
had to be explored. It was
"better." The climate was no
  longer so dry.
    Teenagers who were taken by a thief in
the night
in songs as powerful in feeling
as "For Your Love", "Cover Me"
were sealed from that time on
 to a different purpose. Some of you
might say they were snatched up out of their
home.
Many are still not able to
bring such an early vision
to fruition in this world.
Others have been able to visit
  well, but then they could
  have used anything they
  were given.
Rock & roll, as considered here,
includes sounds
which not all persons can
create. It arises above unto a
seemingly wholly gate which
opens & closes, goes & comes
again until you know that
when you lose, you win

        ***

  Got too much stuff
Don't know how to get rid of it
  can you help me Mama?
    can you help me?

It may seem like a simple problem
like a simple housewife problem
      But I really can't
        get rid of it

Just don't know what to throw away
  what to keep for a later day

      ***

This life is a dream
a rant and a scream
But I'll never join in
I mean to subdue it
To train it on down to its natural size
So it won't overtake me
   I mean to be wise

The dream is the devil if it takes you in
   The dream is the spirit
      if with it you win your dominion
   If using it keeps you from treason
   The rope to climb up from the world into reason

***

A Mental Space

Sometimes forced into the space
where you're supposed to be anyway

You have to have a place where you can go
& meditate & get centered in your body

Remember?

Unheeded warning to an earlier self
   the self of 29 or 35 years caught
   warnings shaped in guilty tears
   in stiff repentance wrought.

   Don't lose the substance
by trying to hold the reflection
   remember the ocean
   remember the stars
   remember the jet plane
   look out for Mars
   remember all the things
      that you've been taught
   but go ahead & do
   the things you've bought
              Try a little
              mixing it
              together

if you chose, you lose
   to the changing weather
   winds pass over
   open field's dry weeds
   How do you order the garden
   if you didn't plant the seeds?

              ***

Sojourney

The girl in the black leather jacket
   off the back of some man's motorcycle
   jumps with her whole suit of armour
   into the pool at Zilker Park

I can see her broad view
   and the smile spread clear across it
   when in childlike pleasure speaking
   she opens up her darkish rosebud mouth

"You blow my mind," says the Cuban lady lawyer
"you tickle my fancy," says the country mouse
"I'm listening," says the preacher's daughter
And we all go over together to her house.
You see it's her 11th anniversary
And she's been making time with the butcher
                      in her kitchen
And her husband, though he doesn't really
                      show it
   thinks she's onto something, & he wants
                      to know it.
She's a little bit fat, but no guilt, forget that
   Free spirit rebuilt with a
                      middle class family

She read my Bob Dylan book out loud
      like I didn't know what I'd been reading
She used to be a nurse
  gave us alka seltzer with mint
              at the end of the evening
You better watch out when you go to
                    her house
    it's not easy leaving
  There's a reclining attitude to
                  every chair

She jumps
  with her black leather jacket
  into the pool at Zilker Park
  I can see her broad view
  & the smile spread across it
  when she opens up in childlike
              pleasure speaking
you see the overlapping teeth
  inside her rosebud mouth.

        ***

The mother cat
  is meowing for her kittens
  wondering where they are

She had moved them
  from the tall grasses over by the
      railroad track
onto the screened porch by the little
            backyard
  while to Florida the people had
        been gone

The mother person home
   cleaned up all the cat droppings
   not liking the smell
  The little Kittens were running
      behind the washing machine
where they thought the children
      couldn't get them very well.

One day the 2 little girls in
          the family
Down to the marketplace with the kitten
            went
& handed them off to people in other
            families
who didn't have enough cats at home
            already

And that night the mother cat
started meowing for her kittens
& for several weeks the meowing
                    kept on
and the people were wondering
  whether it wouldn't be enough
for her to have the grown tiger cat
  from another of her litters
              as a companion

It's the same cat meowing that kills &
        eats birds & lizards
      & toads that the people like to
              have in their garden
That comes up to the mother person
      & rubs against her legs
    every time she goes outside
      to hang up the washing
    & that breaks out the screen
        just after it's been fixed
    & jumps up on the counter
    whenever she can sneak inside

& that has no sense whatsoever
              of obedience
    & sits up & looks out with eyes
          that say
    see what I will do?

and the people come to think the
        tiger tom cat
will be a satisfactory companion

  For after all,
He once was her own
                kitten

      ***

    Two birds flying out over
                    the sky
   One passing the other
then the other passing that
        one by
  Two birds in free southbound
         flying together
    Forewarned by the north winds
       control of the weather

    Annual flight
      chased by the wind
    that would threaten
      their free flying way
          to amend

    Two birds ongoing
    in quiet descending
    on rivers still running
    their thirst still attending
    with wings that enable them
      sooner than men
to go fleeing in freedom the
               uneasy wind

While men toil by each other
      studying & trying
their earthenware ideas
before they go flying

***

"All detail of daily living must be
 rescued from human dominion
 & brought under the gov. of Divine Principle
 if experience is to be held
 secure."

Divine = given or inspired by God

From an article called "Safety" in God's Law of Adjustment book.

Wed.
12/20/89

My love is funny, ya know?
  But it's there
  It drifts in & out of ecstasy
              unaware
It really comes down from up above
   & it's slow
& it's fast
my love   will last.

***

When the lawyer begins to get angry
   He shows that his case is not sure
Until anger, things may have been
                            looking his way
But now he reveals there is doubt
                            he must cure.

If he were convinced of his clients,
   In the face of all efforts to stain
Their veracity & their capacity,
   His assurance would surely remain.
And the lawyer would ride in his saddle,
   Would never jump off & draw sword,
If he's taken his case
   the untruths to efface
Bringing views into even accord.

                        ***

Garbage in World

Sprawling materialism
the decay of which
is impossible to control

1986

Play Scene

<u>WOMAN</u> in scruffy cutoffs, etc.

"It took me so many years to get my clothes together. I don't know what I was thinking."

<u>ANOTHER WOMAN</u> looks at her thinking, "uh, wait a minute, if there's one obvious thing it's that your clothes are not together?"

<u>WOMAN</u> "I mean I used huge chunks of time thinking about measuring up thru clothes, & yet every time I pained myself to go out & do so, I always ended up buying another version of what I already had."

<u>ANOTHER</u> "I don't know where they would have been selling that outfit."

<u>WOMAN</u> "Oh, you know what I mean."

<u>ANOTHER</u> "Everything looked good on me & I loved it all."

***

When he conjured up putting
   the bricks in the bed
I made fun & scowled
I was out of my head
So sweetly he laid them
   upon the black stove
And wrapped them in towels
   so I wouldn't be cold
But I was too old
To enjoy his surprise
I was a blind man
   without any eyes

***

Do you know what you have
> eaten?
Do you know what you have
> said?
Were the American pioneers completely
> living?
Or were they just as we are
> partly dead?

    And we are pioneers
    struggling for our freedom
    over the hills of mind our wagons roll
    trying to prove whatever
        we've been believing

    Balancing the wages
     building on some corner stone
      testing our new lights
       in misty crowds at nights
        checking them out again
         at home
          alone.

***

The carnival beat is in circles of sameness
   my stomach recoils at the thought
For the sideshow's bright prizes, I spend
                          all my money
But when I get home, then
         I hate what I've bought
Swinging a babe in the porch swing on
              Saturday
Brings me the carnival beat

My stomach goes round til it causes me pain
   And in nausea I get to my feet
The pendulum beat of the old attic rocker
   from extreme to the other it moves
The slower it goes, the plainer the thought
   til the carnival ocean it soothes.

                ***

Human Spirit

1. subject to pride—either full of pride or dejected
2. you're walking on your own 2 feet
3. you're interested in "what can I get out of this?" or saying "what can I do?"
4. you're puffed up
5. you condemn
6. you don't see Jesus
7. you fold under persecution
8. you overdirect
9. you strive
10. you approve of war
11. you rate your fellow man & judge him for his weakness
12. you want it all

Holy Spirit

1. poor in Spirit
2. you're leaning on the everlasting arm
3. you're about your father's business
4. you're unafraid
5. you love & understand
6. you see Jesus
7. you grow under persecution
8. you listen before you make your moves
9. you are patient
10. you love peace
11. you know all men are equal & look for every man's gift
12. you share

***

She caused a transplant of my being
   before I got to grow
I felt I had to be like her
   but I couldn't let it show
She moved me onto richer ground
   but I preferred the sand
I couldn't measure up, but still
     I felt a real demand

***

Sleep gives its relief from sin
But then I have to wake up again

***

Texas county courtroom
deputy with criminal
                        suspects
   Thin, fairly young w/gun on
hip walks into courtroom
 sunglasses on
 gold chain around neck
  handcuffs hanging onto
   bullets in belt
  cowboy shirt
   badge on pocket with pens
   sits down
  pulls up ironed jeans
   pulls up already pulled up
                    one stripe socks
            then puts jeans back
                        down
                            around
                        shiny
                        Brown
                        cowboy boot
Then does the same with the
                        other leg
Revealing knife in boot
Cases coming up on 5 men
   who he brought in
   now all sitting up close
                    to judge

Winter '86

The pain of the protein factory
   working all day
   nothing to eat
   nothing to drink except water
   looking down all day
   having to confront only what you have got
          access to through your mind
   while doing the uninteresting work
   keeping moving
you 1st find out that you are nothing
& that you really have no mind
because you can't control it
or make it stay feeling
how you want it to feel

Then you start wondering why you
   have been doing all this
     reading & writing
   & housecleaning at home
If you can't take the feeling of it
   around with you wherever you go
& then you want some way to know the
reality around you
when you are out there
   interacting with other people
while not falling headlong into
        snares & illusions

* * *

You start to wonder whether you
got into this mess on your own
   or were you led to learn?

You remember
   however I got here
   He can get me out

                           ***

In the backrooms
& in the courtrooms

in the shack houses
& electric game rooms
you can't fake it
it's gotta come out naturally

you can't imitate it
  it's gotta happen naturally

There will be mockers
  in the last times
  makin a buck

The cat's gonna meow
    every time
  you go out

You better know it
  what does the cat tell you
  it wants food

it wants affection
& if your latest selection
  has left the cat out

of the structure
the cat meows
so you can remember

***

WORK =

Mir: the earnest effort
     to complete a specific task
     w/out fainting
     or having the boss say
          "not good enough"

Mark: "getting the job done"

***

Every day is different on its own
    You don't have to strain to make it
Open up your child-heart thought
    This advice is good if you'll take it

***

If destinations, one on one,
   piled inside the chests of years
   Bring a sense of work well done
   then I will know elation

          ***

My sisters were made with a moderate mold
   middle of the road
   will they grow old?

I'll stay young until I die
   tho die I really don't plan to

        Hi

        ***

Secrets are important
   If you keep it to yourself
You can go around the world
   As though you were a man-sized elf

***

I'm not a ready to go type of girl
& I never have been
I came onto this earth this way
& I have to deal with it
There are various ideas I work with
in order to become this ready to go type
but none of them ever really succeeds

For instance, looking right to
   myself is practically
   impossible. And how can a person
Go without looking right to
himself?

Then there's the comfort factor,
How can I leave if I haven't
managed to get to the comfort
level yet?

Also, how can a person stand to
leave the house in disorder?
And there are always these
lights to turn off & that toothpaste
that has to be rinsed out of Mark's
toothbruth & off the sink
where he has just brushed his teeth
(THANK GOD)

12/8/94

    O great burden of
        the ages
as I move my floor desk
      from the wall
To over in front of the
        window
I lay you partly
    down

***

Man & Wife In Old Truck At Quick Stop

His chin above her glasses
close side by side they drove
I saw them from my driver's seat
when we were on the road
I parked right next up to them
Their pick-up truck was red
I really wanted to draw them, but
I'm writing this instead

Their faces & their freckles
years of sun did show
The way he spit, the way she sat
Hinted they might be hard to know
Away they drove, as I went in
some Sunday beer to buy
The moon was there when I came out
We can make it if we try.

***

How do we know so little?
We know what we can prove
The scientist takes his dreams
              into the lab
  from out of the blue
  the walks alone, from time to time
  His thoughts in doubt ascending
  the path the other later go
  on his frontier depending

***

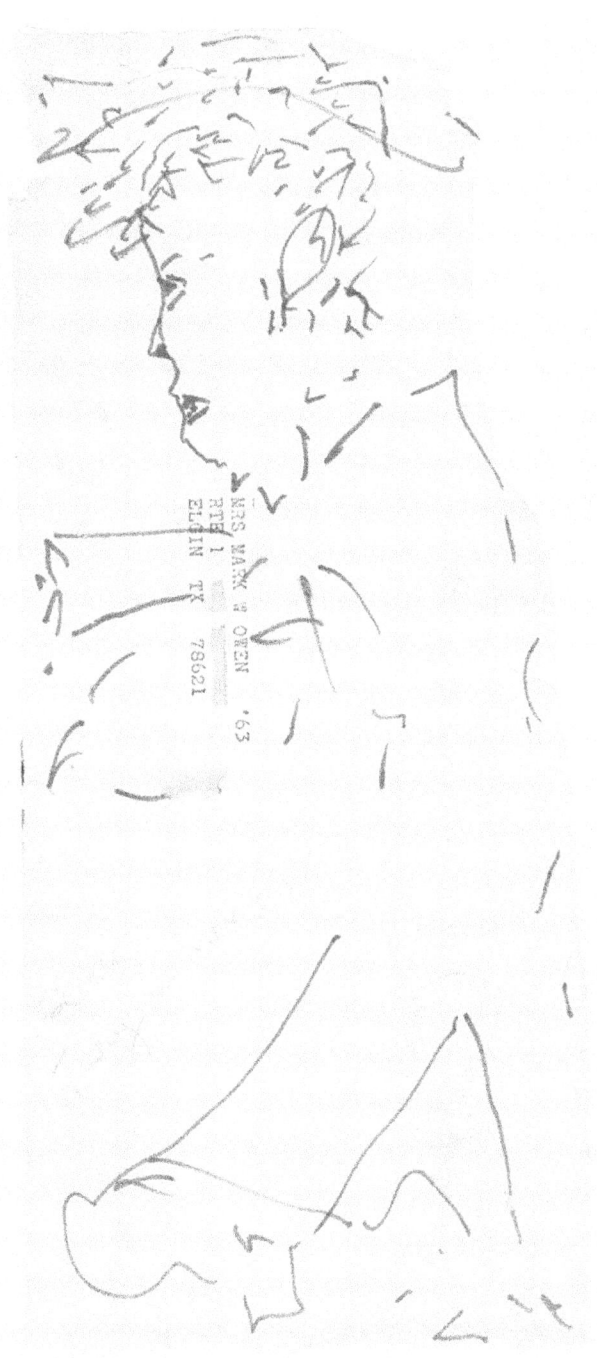

Images, images
  forget all the images
Give yourself a chance to live
    Breathe, breathe
Breathe all the visions
 Give them a chance to be
Why do you talk if you can't
      talk to me?
Can you verify thought
  playing back to yourself?
  Test on the outside
   study within
  Prove out your visions
  if life you
    would
     win

***

Those little shoes
   Made me smile
In the childhood of my children
A harbor in the midst of mild
                              oppression
They would stay beneath
  the spare chair of the kitchen
Or move often in the middle of the floor
 So you could trip on them
  as you came through the door

                ***

2 things which lead you out of looking with material eye:

1) When you look at your body, find it unpleasing, & can't change it yourself
2) When you find yourself in unpleasing circumstances

The conclusion in both cases is: There must be more here than meets the naked eye.

> That is, if God is good…
> if there is any hope…
> if life is worth living…
> if true love…

***

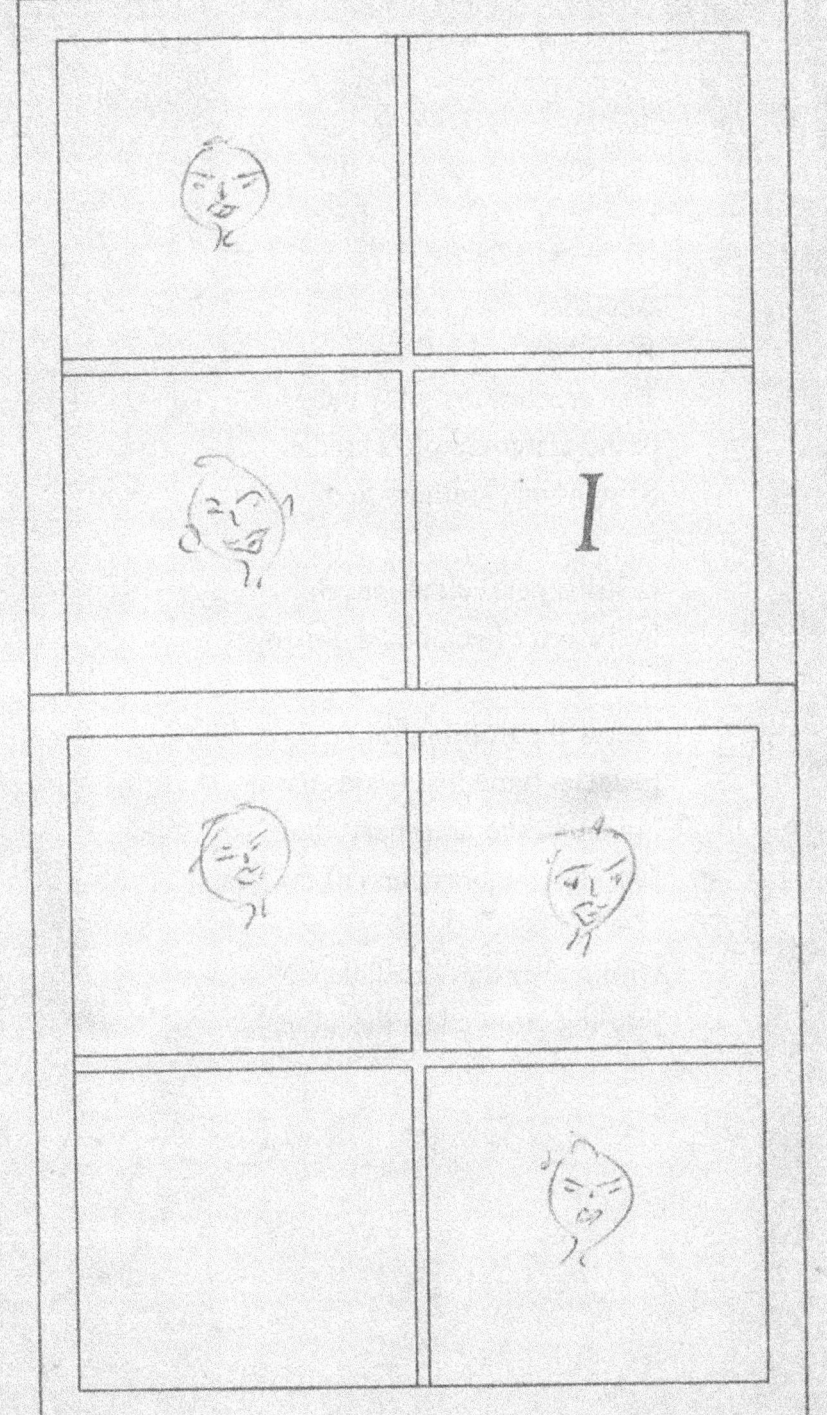

Abortion

Why the lilied lullaby
That soothes my silky baby,
In the crater temple's cradle,
Brings back softness to my eyes,

Is still a pearl cloud puzzle
In the urn of smoothed goodbyes.

Below the trolling traitor skys
Erupts a fume that braids me—
For some sad hour pervading,
Through the brashness of my years,

Oiling over that lost father
Smiling crooked smiles of tears.

9/67

Honest to God
I think I see more of Jesus
in riding my big daughter's bike
  with my little daughter
  than I do
  going to church
    on Sunday morning

***

So astutely you disarmed me
    of my old conspicuous pride
I knew at once I'd have you
    If to me you'd be allied.
Your bare essential foot from
    way across the room I spied.
I asked my friend, "Who
    is that?"
"It's my cousin," he replied.
"Oh, John, you mean your
    life with country cousin
    has been cast?
This is the only kind I'll
    find with whom my
    love might last."

***

My Drawing of Marie

Analyzing relationships
   is a drag
Why does everybody go around
     Doing it?
  The thing that's fun
    is living the Truth
  Not lounging around
     removing it

***

Know your own place
   within the race
Then those balls you'll better
              field
You aren't out front to
      preach the word
You're walking to be healed
playing in the left field
  & yeah that is a talent
you need to do what you can do
  Because the team can't do
    without it.

***

Mike at the Filling Station

I was still under five
blue shirt, work shirt
station on the corner
across the street & down 2 blocks
   from our house
a clean & tidy place
   too far to see from our house
   too far to walk alone
I went hours to bed that night
& remembered how to get there.

***

Life Shines

   Shadow is cast
   How to reclaim
     from the infinite
         past

***

From the minute you wake up
  until you lay down back
      in your bed
lay down
lay down
lay down

Misled?
  Get out of bed
  Keep y'self fed
  use your head

Don't get bored
You've got a sword
you'll get no award
but you won't be ignored

Where we gonna get it?
  you gotta just let it
  color alphabet it
  if you can't cigarette it

Old stove smoke it
  if it won't start
    choke it

Or else get off that
  broken down horse
  oh…of course…

A Kind of Two-faced

is showing a different activity w/people
  than when you let it happen naturally when
you are alone
    & relatively unconcerned about what another
            person may think of you
  (possibly totally oblivious to sense of other
     which is really great freedom in a way
                But…)
  Sometimes a mask might be more the true
  you than the way you appear to be

   if it expresses hope instead of the dumb
    acceptance of a condition not yet overcome

***

Subdivision Swimming Pool

The Holy Ghost
is a different kind of Ghost
No, we really can't exactly figure it out
    when it comes upon us.
I mean really now, THE HOLY GHOST, can
    this be true?
At least I'm not self-conscious when
  this thing I'm speaking of happens,
    how about you?
Although I am responsible for my motions
 & aware of everything I say
 & conscious of what others do, & in a
    non-critical way
Oh come on now — hey — what is the
 HOLY GHOST?
 is it this weird feeling that's been coming
    upon me every day,
everybody looking better instead of worse
everybody looking like a blessing instead of
    a curse?
I find this refuge when I take
 the kids over to the pool
 & I just sit & watch
But I'm feeling like this state of mind
 could be easily shaken
if I let my mind drift off into imagination

They come up on the television
    Rustlin' & 'a raisin'
    Prancin' & 'a praisin'
    Feastin' & 'a gazin'
They haven't got the word
It's just evangelistic fever
Spreading its judgmental germ
    and mudding up the river.

***

<u>Salvation</u>

Drink of the water
of your own salvation
Drink of the wine of the
          cross
You carry it on
   when you find no base
       station
   your gain is in your loss.

The son of man
   has no place to rest his head
  Unlike the birds of the air have a nest.
Unlike the foxes have their holes,
  only in walking
     Right on
     can he rest.

Matt 10:38-39

If in this world
   ya just can't make it
   Don't fake it
     sister

   Don't ever compare yourself
   to what has struck ya sore

   Believe me sister
     If you let a better look distract you
you'll never see the end you're travelin' for

   if in the world
    ya just can't make it
    forget it
      sister

The other world
   is worth the dyin', & dyin'
       & dying some more

Sister, sister
   Don't let it all distract you
or you'll never see the end you've been
             travelin'
                for

           ***

Who Am I?

Holding on to the reality of experience
   I can easily remember from the time
           of being small
It is hard to distinguish the "old man"
From the "new man," what they call.
The false man, from the true man,
it's just confusing to think about it
         anymore
And I think I'm going to drop it
  because I feel like I already
          know

***

After a rather startling event,
Which triggered several major alterations,
They found that they had somehow
                          started
To erase the fragile fabric of their
                          love.
Yet within it they still tried to dress,
For fear of obliging a further
                          sacrifice
Of closeness in space.

The shallowness of being sandwiched
In between sheets of coarser
                          weaving than before
Was minor price to pay
For sanguine satisfaction
                          scored within malaise

Belied the passing days,
Of chosen gestures and varied
To regain the status quo
And infinite the woe
Of planning sighed real reactions
That had primed themselves
                          short time ago.

                                             '67?

    For Mark
myself, whatever that is, will never
say yes to things I used to find
  enticing before

His hand,
If wood sired elderberries won't enhance
        themselves in glasses
with expensive crystal stems
will linger

I feared
  to lose impediments of overwoven webs
when spiders were still allowed in my
        closet to linger for spinning
Now Deeper
There are crops planted so numerous
As to displace whims which would
        have called before
If he had left me

              ***

I was thinking about baskets
  all woven like smocking
   I was thinking about lying down
I was thinking about walking
   Bears in their girdles
   red bearded & lean
   pears running hurdles
   on some good king's green
When in through the doorway
   that leads to my chamber
   loped two white haired horses
   from the snows of December
   Beckoning, taking for granted
                I'd ride
But for truth in my thought
   I retreated to hide
   If they were some old paints
   then I might be tempted
   to leave my vocation
   assume it had ended
But, blazing the white there
   no soldier they've lended
   a way to ride out
   of his dream world extended
What happens to horses,
                all white

when they hit mud?
What happens to ideals
        all white
when they meet blood?
What happens to soldiers
  when they become saints?
They end their long walk
  on the back of old paints

#1

Once I went to a church & they told me
the streets of heaven are lined with gold
Once I heard a song & it said
I hear the streets of heaven are
                     all lined in gold
I liked the songs they were singing
But a little bit later I got to thinking
It sure does seem cold,
                    streets lined with gold
Once I read a book & it told me
  if you bear the cross, then you'll wear the crown
Once I heard a wise friend say
  you're gonna make it if
    you keep your wheels going 'round
I believed them when I heard
but a little later I got to thinking
what am I going to do when the
  sun goes down,
wearing a crown
     with wheels goin round?

#2

Do you listen
  to the toothless stroller
wandering on the road?
Or say to yourself, as your two ways pass
  He's ugly & he's old?
Does he have a tale to tell you
that may be worth your precious minute?
Does it matter what he says
  to you? Can you see
  the substance in it?
Only after it's grown
  will you own what on the road you've sown
Give your seeds to the sunburn & pain
  Give them away to the wind & rain
  But watch them just for fun
Many be the seeds I've sown
  But few of the seeds I've tended
And my old clothes are worn to bare
  through having thrice been mended
How many times must I mend my clothes
  Before I let them go?
Through how many shapes must
     the new thought pass
Before true form will show?

                #3

    as for patterned response
I can't see that at all
  hit me with your battered sconce
    & walk me quicko down the hall
 you may wish that
      that was all   AMEN
—But that's not all…
I'm the Cinderella at my mother's ball
  so sail me down the river
  mail me until I quiver
  nail me & feed me liver
 I'm not ready to give her up
—

  Not ready to deliver
So let me drink my shattered cup
  & sail me on down the river
  sail me   sail me
  sail me on down
  sail me on down the river
  paint me a clown on top of my
                  frown
& sail me on down the river.

#4
1979

While I was thinkin about a rabbit
   thinkin about a clown
   a man came along
   his face lookin down
   he was carrying the basket
     all woven with smocking
     the basket was empty
   that's why he was looking

Men are on trial
   men are at ease
   men are restricted
   men do as they please

Put something in his basket
   all woven with smocking
   so he won't have to continue
   his everyday looking
   searching for fruits
     eyeing the weeds

Walking in ponds, way up to the knees
   partial to Abraham
   partial to Lot
  But not really knowing
   just what it is he's got.

#5
1979

I left my home
down on my Daddy's farm
before I went away.

Since then
I've been learning
what I'm trying to learn —
if you know you'd better go
then you better not stay —
Because you'll get in your
way, that way.

I left my Mama
But I knew I'd come back
She wash & folds my laundry
& she lays it in a stack.
You can rest at her feet
  before the next attack
if you can't make it
you still know she'll be there later
she's a white waiter,
  married to an ice skater.

#6

I'd rather just make history
    than learn about it
   any old day

But can you do it
    without learning
  what the others had to say?

***

Forgive me now, the rose of sharon takes me
                                    back so far
Unto a time my earth was guided
                                  by an inner star
A living light within me burned
  no tribulation did I feel
The latter day affliction
     hadn't shown itself
     for me to heal
Laid in summer's heat, unclothed
The temptor had not spoken
A child of innocence did own
the faith it had not broken

June 6, '76

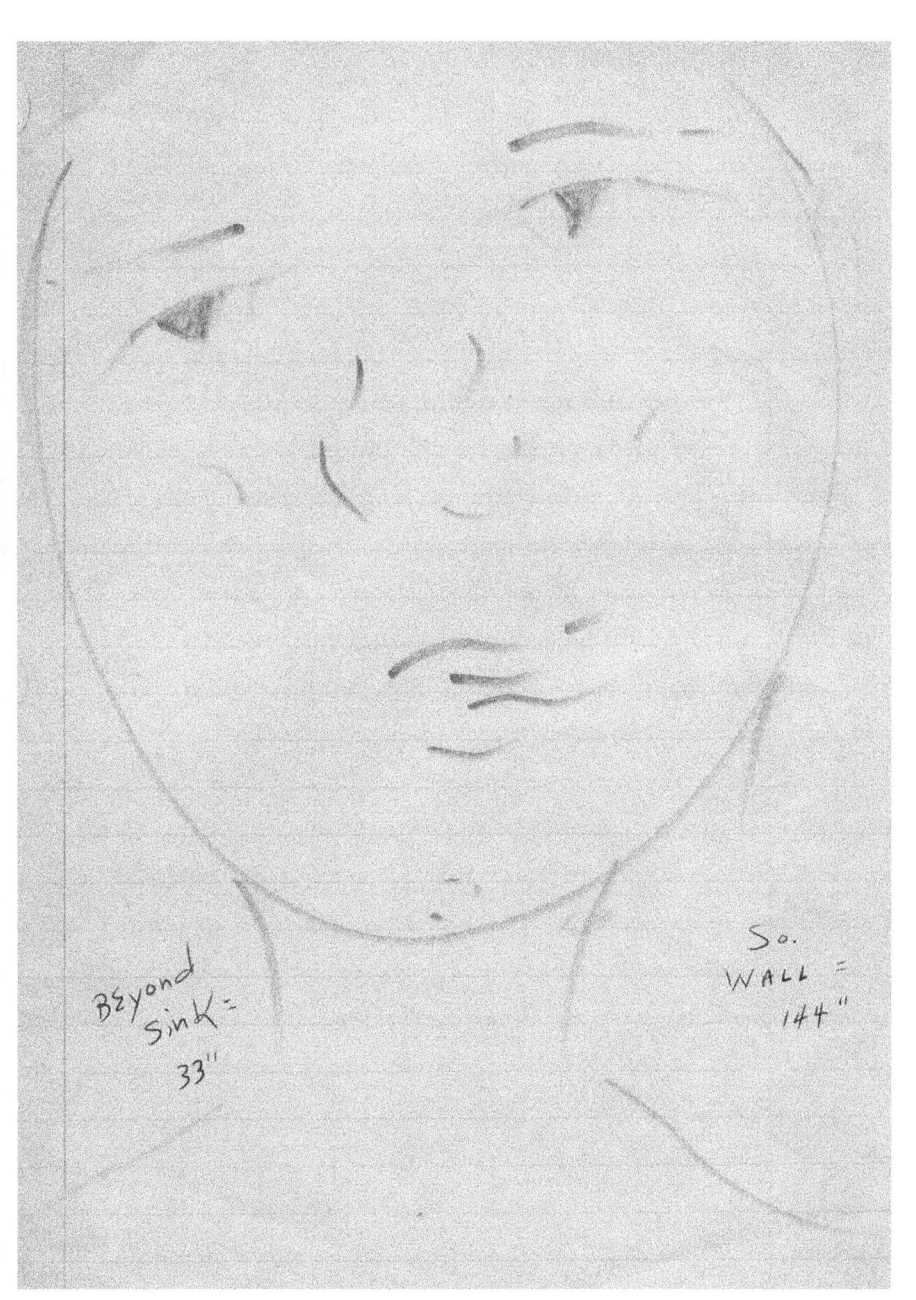

Look at the sea with a sailor's eye
  who's sighting for the land
You wouldn't stop on cannibal isle
  or anchor on a strand.
You wouldn't settle for a desert either
  if your ship could get you further
But closer blows the hurricane
  and you can't sail forever…

Memory of Summer 1971

You plan yourself out well
  you won't hear the Truth knock
The Truth will soon come to your door as a
                                      stranger
If you are a stranger
  You might as well wander
A house fully furnished
  is no less a danger

***

When you find out you're not
  what you thought you were (again)
  you just have to get out there & try
  not really knowing exactly who you are
  & somehow it will turn out like it's
              supposed to
    you can be sure
if you just keep faith in
  the spirit that led you
to find out what you weren't
  in the first place

              ***

We have to learn to accept
ourself in all the
circumstances of life. If
we can't accept something
about ourself, then we
should take that as a clue
to change it. We can't
love others w'out loving
ourself. To love yourself is
not to admire or adore your
self, but to be grateful
for your individual manifestation
& to be able to have
nothing to hide. If I can
stand naked (so to speak*) in
body & spirit, then I can
accept my own lot &
communicate with others.
If I am ashamed of myself
to myself, then I have to
find out what I am
thinking or doing that is

making me feel this
guilt or sense that I am
unworthy & trash it from
my life.

    & this ain't easy

10.18.05

Hard core last days stuff. ✞

* *Standing naked does not involve your letting people in the bathroom while you take care of whatever you have to do there by yourself. It involves only your revealing of your ideas. And this is the hardest thing to do. Because, they will not accept these ideas.*

we came to earth to be bowled
over
not to insure that our opinions
   are right
we came into the world to
    unfold together
not to remain as a seed
        so tight

1/20/95

One time I read a thing about an oriental family
all (men) in the family were healers
   but on different levels
it was something about
   the speaker's next older brother would heal thru knife
   the even older brother would heal thru herbs
   the dad would heal a person as he heard him
              manifest a thought
             through his words
  & the granddad would heal merely by
            his presence

                ***

Old for the new
  false for the true
  you think about me
I'll think about you
  Holy Spirit
   coming through
  by ♡ to ♡
   brother to brother

       ***

Everyone has to find something he wants to
do & do it   .   or else life is not
worth living ,   & a man loses hope

Freedom, to an extent, consists in
finding something you want to do
& doing it
& after finding a way to do it
being able to keep on doing it
in the face of people telling you
you shouldn't do it
& that you should do what they
   think instead
      so don't.

***

Redemption
    means
  there is a place for you
to work & watch & wait at the same time
and you can take it with you
where ever you go

(or whoever arrives at the door)

                   ***

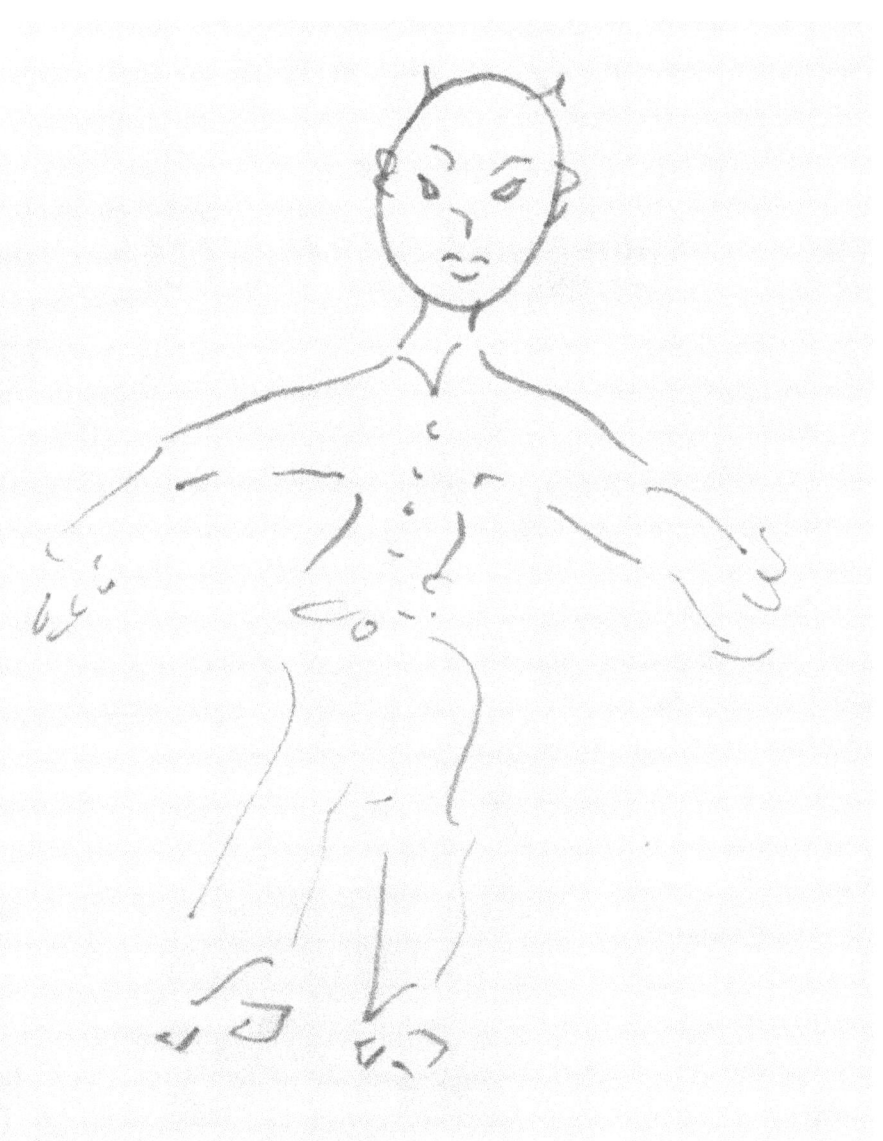

in search of
the perfect pair of shoes

To Todd,

Who gave me a beautiful notebook to write in and gave me freedom to say something to him on paper w'out putting me down.

Chapter 1

We pulled into the
garage at our
house in Houston, Texas.

It was darker in
there than when
we had been driving
home from the
dancing lesson.

As usual, the rolling
of the car caused me
an unwillingness to
get out.

I looked at the
new ballet slippers
on my feet.

To myself I said,
"No way I'm going
to be wearing these
anymore."

Thank God I got
outta that one
early.

When you find out
something you don't
want to wear,
you don't wear it
again.

Chapter 2

Next time was a little bit the opposite. I wore my moccasins to church & Betsy said, "Look, you don't want to be wearing those to church!"

Well, I just stopped going to church. But I kept wearing my moccasins.

Chapter 3

That Chapter 2 deal
turned out to be
a pretty good
thing. Then, on
Sundays I did
not need to
bother my husband
anymore.

& it was a lot more
relaxing to let
him bother* me
than to go to
church…

    Amen

Chapter 4

One time when I was
wearing my boots
with a dress outfit
I just took them
off & went bare
footed for awhile
& then it was
easy to put them
back on again.

Boots

Chapter 5

Flip Flops
were my favorite
& about only shoes
for awhile.

But, if you are a
person who trips up
every once in awhile,
that will happen at
the most inappropriate
time & you will be
blamed for all kinds of
things you did not
ever do. Watch out
for Flip Flops.

Chapter 6

Boots are
the best I can
recommend so
far, because they
are easily removed
unto one's bare
feet, which are
adequate to any
occasion, except
war, & whooah
I will not do that
& if I was caught I'd
have on Boots
anyway, so…

Flip Flops are OK
for the house and market,
but that's pretty
much their limit
for a workin girl.
Now, if you're rich &
on vacation on a
boat or resort,
then they're appropriate.
(Always have your Boots
 at hand tho)

Chapter 7

Rick Nalle lived with Mark
& me for awhile before
he & Betsy got married.
Rick came down to Texas
from a Main Line Philadelphia
family, & he wanted to
be a cattle rancher.

He told me that when
you're looking to plan
out your life occupation
you just ask yourself "what
do I like to wear?" & then
you take it from there.
I said, "Rick, that's Tom
Foolery, it's just the
opposite."

The understanding which comes
with years has proved

him right.

Chapter 8

The thing I was meeting
up with about the idea
was this tonite: I'm
having to go to West Virginia
with Mark, & I don't
really want to go.
But the angst of having
him go w'out me super-
imposes on the fear
I have of having to
fly on an airplane
(2011!) & also of
having to super-
socialize. At least
I don't have to worry
about what shoes I
have on in W. VA.
That's a Godsend.

So, anyway, what shoes
am I gonna take?
To keep with the
theme of this
Book—

    Boots, Flip Flops,
moccasins. However,
the most important
addition to those 3
is: The Walking
        Shoes

No problem. I've
got those, because I
walk with Mark
all the time.

Which ones will
I pick?
(problems of abundance)

Why do I have so
   many pairs of
shoes?

Duh.

Because, as I already
told you, I am
in search of the
perfect pair of
   shoes!

Chapter 9

Well, the next thing
that happened was
I needed to go to
West Virginia again with
Mark on the airplane,
that I did not
want to ride.

Which pair of Boots
was I gonna take?

Well, we had Scott &
Linda coming & they
were gonna get all
dressed up to do
whatever in Pittsburgh.
So I had to take
an outfit for
that. So that
defined the pair of
Boots I had to take
& so that defined
the whole deal.

So, then where
are you left
when you have to
think of your whole
life in terms of
one pair of boots,
what are you
going to do?

Well, they better
be comfortable.

And then, you
build your whole
wardrobe around
them. Why not?

Well, I thought
about that awhile
longer, & then
it came to me
that you can
carry another
pair of boots in
your suitcase if
you don't have
another big pack
of textiles inhibiting
the space. So, it
is possible to have 2
pairs of Boots.

However, in that case, one of
the 2 pairs needs to be able
to be used with shorts.

Now, we are talking about
what happens in the long
run. (not a marathon competition)
No competition at any time.
   (unless you like it that much)

And if you do, of course you
are a complete loser, because
obviously you can't win without there being a loser.
So losers must exist in
order for you to win.
Unless, you just play

solitaire. And in that
case, there's ol' Sol.

Well, when you go to a
wedding, there's a lot
of people, & you like
to see them all. But,
when there are so many
people around that
you don't normally see
that much, it gets to
throw you off balance.
These are times when I
try not to drink too much.
Because, although I hate
being totally sober at these
occasions, I also don't
want to go stumbling
around.   (wear
                    boots)

Really, Flip Flops are
for FLA, boat trips,
for completely protected
areas without a lot of
dirt. And a lot of
natural water, like
the Guadalupe River,
which I can say
if you rent a spot
you will be totally
happy for awhile.

Chapter 10

Actually, I have 4 or 5 pairs
of Boots. & I love them all.
They are appropriate to different
human situations, which I
must endure for awhile.
& I'm not like trying to get
out of it too soon. But, just
before I get to be a burden
on my family.

               When I go there,
I know the Boots I would
wear. I will pick them
up & go. They don't go
with any dresswear.
They with my body,
my soul, & my spirit,
dressed in my night-
wear — my panties,
& a little bit of t-shirt
covering my upper
breasts. That's what
I would go in, God,
to meet you in the
great Beyond.

Chapter 11

I awake to a new day,
   always. Thank you,
      me' Lord

One thing I know
for sure is this:
you do not take your
family problems into a
ball park. And, anybody
who tempts you to do
so, you tell him,
check me out later on
that one, brother, but
not in the ball park.
Period. The end.
   I'll take my shoes
off on that one any
day.

6/10/2011

Chapter 12

When I once tried to reduce my #'s of pairs of shoes to ①, Weezie showed up, by surprise as usual, sitting in the porch swing, as we returned from a trip to Austin. I said, "I thought you said you were not coming after all," and she said "surprise!" Of course I hate surprises, but I also do not like going with whatever happens. When she asked what I'd been thinking about lately, I told her I'd mostly been working around the house & yard, but my main philosophical concern was how to narrow down my number of shoes. She said, well, you don't want to narrow it down too much, because it is better for your feet to be exposed to different styles.

Chapter 13

One time when I went
over to my nephew's
house when he lived
off 34th St. in Austin
& he turned out not
to be there after all,
we (Mark & me) just
stood out on his porch
& put the package away
from any more rain
that might come. & did
not go inside since he
turned out not to be
there, but I noticed
about 6 pairs of boots
on the porch, & they were
all turning over & wet,
& I was wondering
if there might be
another person in my
family in search of
the perfect pair of
shoes, even harder
than I had been
doing.

Chapter 14

There's sometimes
where you take
your shoes off
& you just let it go

That was one time
where it was I let
Todd in to know
the interesting
thing that really
only I knew
about the keeping
of the appetite
unto the true blue.
But it is a tale to bring
something more in view.
There is a shoe that can be worn
that never wears down
whether you wear it in the woods
or in any kind of town
"this shoe is sure around"
Do you know what that means?
It is that you no longer
 have to use screens.

You still have a shoe
and it's the one you have on.
It never betrayed
only took you along.
If this shoe now is shabby
and looks at an end
it only will turn you
unto your next friend.
If the shoe should happen
to just fall apart
consider it a trade toward
the craft of your art.

Those boots that you left
on your old tours back,
you have swamped all their messages
out of the sack
and dividends paid you
way past your belief
which will benefit you later
—to your relief

OK, Todd, here I go again…

Weezie & me are sitting in the station
waiting for someone in the
family to arrive. (oh God, finally
the activity has ceased for awhile
I take out my book & start
to read) "Oh no, Miriam, we
can't do that. We take the time
together to chat   !"

I close my book. "OK, tell
me a story."

She did. And she
"expanded" on it, as they
say. It was a lot of fun to
listen to her, but inaccuracy
isn't a thing I'm really into,
maybe that's why I'm so boring,
 oh well. But, telling a
story as it really happened,
why can't that be interesting
enough?

Oh Todd, this is a hard
thing for me to write again.
Mark & I have had another
fight. It's because I said
it didn't matter to me what
he watched, I would be
interested. Well, ya can even
be in trouble for that.
There's no way to not be
in trouble.

We must be able to express
ourselves in some way

w'out getting into trouble,
  No?

Well, with Mark you
either have to go with
exactly what he says,
or you are in trouble.

I really don't care,
because I love Mark,
& I want to be as
he wants me to be.
But, of course I can't.

Because, I must, at all cost,
  be myself.
    But, who am I?

I am, says God.
I exist say I. What am I
gonna do about it, say I?

Well, I'm gonna start a
sister soiree where we can
all keep in touch.
    That's working.

As my husband is concerned,
I say, well, I'm going to
speak to him clearly about
ideas. That has not yet
worked. But, I think it
is a possibility, if I
keep on trying. That
does not mean that I am
thinking I'm a big deal.
It's just that I don't
understand why he does not

understand why my thinking
  is real.

I am getting rid of another
pair of shoes, that Susan
Adams wanted when she
saw them on my feet.
That's kind of fun to
give somebody something
they wanted that you
had, & could not give
them until you had
another pair of shoes
to replace them.

Todd, I know it's sort
of hard to stay with me
on this. But take it,
take it as a kiss. Please
don't scorn it, &, as many
have done before, call me
scornful, because…
   I'm worth much more.

Todd, I'm not reading this
back as I start again. But
here I am, your true blue
Mir.

I have an experience
that I've dealt with by
drinking alcohol.
(some people just drink
straight vinegar)
& so do I every once
in awhile.

Anyway, my natural

choice is beer. I've
found a bit of a snip of
gin is OK, but I've never
bought more than a ½ pt.
Because, if I did, I'd
drink too much.

I did this when my
parents were faltering
& I cleaned their
house & went out there
      once a week.

I drove to Lakeway once
a week to do this, &
I found my Dad needing
a lot of body work.
Which body work I
did. Then, I had
to drive back home.
I needed something.
I took a bit o' the gin,
I went back home,
where awaiting me
was my own housework,
cooking, & paperwork.
I could not keep up.
  I felt it was OK
to take this tranquilizer.
It was.

I don't know about your
problems w/alcohol,
but I've heard of
them. It's not my
business to get into
details about you
shared with me.

I am no meddler.

What I do know is that
I love & adore you.
You are a wonderful
person in life as
we know it. I care
about you a lot.
I have a lot of problems
to deal with
that you will never
know about. (unless you
ask) I am always
here for you if you
want to talk.
I don't think you
want to, tho.

Sometimes I think
your problem (if
you have one) is that
it is hard to talk
to anyone. It's my
problem. (That's
probably the reason I
think it might be
your problem; of
course, I don't know.)

Again today, somebody
noticed my shoes, &
said, "I like those
pair of shoes."

I said, "What's
your size, I'll get
you a pair."

He said, "How long have you had those?"
I said, "About 20 years, but I know how to get you a pair if you want them"
The longer I go on this freewheeling book, the more I want to give it to you. Maybe you can read it at a time there is nothing else to do but take another drink. It's hard, Todd.

But we can do it. We can still drink our beer, and we are not alcoholics. We have chosen to overuse a good medicine. But we…I don't exactly know.

By the way, thanks a lot for ushering me out of that venue at Toby's wedding. Thank you. I needed you, & you helped me.

***

    Here I stand, in my
      perfect pair
         of
       SHOES

P.S. The perfect pair
of shoes are the ones
you're already in.

If not, get rid of them.
If they're the only
pair of shoes you've
got, ya better not.

Dear Todd,

I have to tell you
about this latest funny
thing. Like, Mark & I
squeeze the toothpaste
tube in a different way
from each other. When
he thinks it's done, I
get a new one for him
& then I use the old
one for about a month
longer. Ya get it?
However, I have no
problem whenever
he says he needs one.

I wanted to tell you the
story of when I first
met Mark. (I know you
have never liked it
that we fought & yelled
at each other.)

But, I wanted to write
my story down about
this, & I do believe
that these writings
in this book are not
uninspired by my
own honesty before God.

Allison & I met John
at the wedding of
Lynn Smith & an
Italian guy—they

all went to Principia
College together.

Alli & I were sitting
at a swimming pool at
the Floeter's house
in Piney Point Village,
one of the 5-7 villages
incorporated by my
Dad, which still exist.

We were sitting there, & we
saw a big black taxi drive
up, & a guy got out of
the taxi, & came walking
directly out to the pool.
We looked at him, & we
said, Wooooh! He came
up & said his name was
John Russell. We said,
"Glad ta meet cha!"

From that time on we 3
were best friends.
   (Allison was in love with him
       But she was wild.)

He was a few years older
than she, & he had a
long way to go.

Anyway, we remained
friends, & eventually
one day when my Mom
made me take Betsy
in with her friend
   to Aquafest,

even tho I didn't
particularly want to
because my best friend
from Birmingham, Alabama
was staying with me
& we had other plans,
we went, & Allison
said, "Oh, Miriam,
we can go by John's
house, because he has
a surprise for you."

I said, Oh well, OK.
What is the surprise?

She said, "I don't know."
We went.

I walked in John's
door on 24th St. I said,
"So what's the big
surprise anyway, John?"

John laughs & points
to the big brass bed
(which belonged to Bo,
who was off in Mississippi
working for his uncle
Bill Drienhofer, I think,
or maybe another uncle)
So John points to the
bed where this guy
in blue jeans with no
shirt lies with his feet
up on the brass bed ends
& a big smile on his
face & a phone in his
hand.

I said, "Who's that &
who's he talkin' to?"

"His mother."

John says, "That's
my cousin Mark
from West Virginia
& he's talking to his
mother," John with
a big laugh says.
"Stick around Miriam."

I could tell you alot
more, but I don't want
to bore you.

***

Super Bowl Sunday 2012

Dear Todd,

I do not believe that all
alcohol talk is erroneous,
incorrect, or off the mark.
Writing under the influence
of alcohol, is what I mean, as
well as speaking out inappropriately
or whatever a person ends
up doing.

My purpose to send you
this book is that you
gave it to me, & for so
many years I've torn
up most of my writing
because of the transitional
case I've been experiencing
was so unclear to me that
I felt it wasn't worthy
of perpetuating it.

However, a writer, a
thinker, a good friend,
must be able to express
himself, to himself, to
the paper, & to his
friend. I certainly don't
expect you to keep this
book. I need it back
for my own exploration
into self-knowledge.

I'm sorry if I messed
up the beautiful book
you brought me, but

please understand
that it has been a
huge relief for me
to share my own
frailties with you
& let you then hand
them back, for my
own edification.

This is a great gift
you have given to
me, & you can
write in the open
pages, or, when you
hand it back to me
I will continue to
expand on my search
for the perfect pair
of shoes.

          ***

Sorry Todd, I just can't keep from
writing, because there's not any
thing in here I wouldn't like to
read again, as I read it over.
It's me. & I'm OK. Not perfect
in any way, but why not say
what I want to say in a way
I would naturally say it?

Can't fake it with you
wouldn't want to
Because then you'd talk back
& I would have to react
put on a subconscious act
& we wouldn't ever come to
what we really want to do
I can't fake it with you.

***

Thief In the Night

Error has been a friend of mine
I've known him all my life
He's offered me a lot of fun
But it all has come to strife

When strife has been your habit
Then the end you must beware
You've made yourself an easy set up
  for the devil's final dare.

***

Once you join forces
   you don't look back
put your own shoes on
    and don't attack
You've got Jesus as your
               witness
Again, don't look back
For sure, not to repeat
   myself,
There will be another hack
But, peace be with you
is the cause to bear
just feel lucky not to
be nailed to a cross
in your underwear

               ***

Another story of the perfect
pair of shoes, is one day
when I used to keep care of
Jack. We were in a store in
Elgin, I don't remember which
one, but I was going in to
get a mop, broom, or vacuum
cleaner bag, or something
I needed of that sort. He was
3½ or 4. He said, "Can I go
& look around?" I said, "Yes,
but keep your eye on me." He
came back to tell me he had
found something that he
wanted. I said, "OK, go
show me." He took me to
a little pair of boots he liked.
Of course, I bought them for
him. He wore them a lot
while he was over here, but
he never would take them
home. Eventually, one of the
zippers broke. I got it
fixed, but soon he grew out
        of them.

***

Thank you God for helping me live in the "world." Even tho I am not "of the world."

Thank you God for my loving husband, Mark Owen.

***

Bob Dylan

Dear Bob,

See the thing was that I was drawing a picture of Bob Dylan out of my mind, and then when I turned it over, to me, it looked like Woodie Guthrie.—

That's Art.

Mortality

You can't run away

But you can always
continue the search
for the perfect pair
of shoes.

....

Although I'm still
looking for the
perfect pair of
shoes, I have
found that a
friend who always
answers the telephone
might be more
important.

no more searching
I'm through.

***

Miriam Owen lives in Elgin, Texas.
This is her first book.

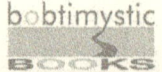

www.ingramcontent.com/pod-product-compliance
Lightning Source LLC
Chambersburg PA
CBHW020934090426
42736CB00010B/1132